Next Generation Physical Science and Everyday Thinking

Unit M

Developing a Model for Magnetism

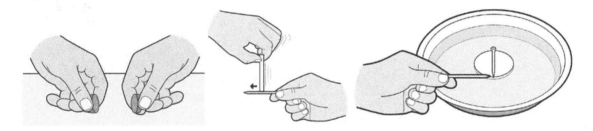

Activate Learning®

Next Gen

PETLC

Lecture-style Class

Next Generation Physical Science and Everyday Thinking

Unit M

Developing a Model for Magnetism

Lecture-style slides

Major support for the development of *Next Gen PET* came from the National Science Foundation Grant No. 1044172 and the Chevron Corporation

© 2018 San Diego State University Research Foundation

human energy·

Activate Learning
44 Amogerone Crossway #7862
Greenwich, CT 06836
www.activatelearning.com

Next Generation Physical Science and Everyday Thinking (*Next Gen PET*)
© 2018 San Diego State University Research Foundation
Licensed exclusively to Activate Learning.

Printed and bound in the United States of America.

ISBN 978-1-68231-337-4
5th Printing
5   22 21 20

This project was supported, in part, by the National
Science Foundation under Grant No. 1044172. Opinions
expressed are those of the authors and not necessarily those
of the National Science Foundation.

Next Gen PET Development Team

Co-authors of Next Gen PET

Fred Goldberg, San Diego State University
Stephen Robinson, Tennessee Technological University
Danielle Harlow, University of California at Santa Barbara
Julie Andrew, University of Colorado at Boulder
Edward Price, California State University at San Marcos
Michael McKean, San Diego State University

Contributed to Development of Materials

Leslie Atkins, Boise State University

Field Test Collaborators

David Mitchell, California Polytechnic University at San Luis Obispo
Anne Marie Bergen, California Polytechnic University at San Luis Obispo
Lola Berber-Jimenez, California Polytechnic University at San Luis Obispo
Nancy Stauch, California Polytechnic University at San Luis Obispo
Tina Duran, California Polytechnic University at San Luis Obispo
Chance Hoellwarth, California Polytechnic University at San Luis Obispo
Paula Engelhardt, Tennessee Technological University

Technical Support

Shawn Alff, San Diego State University Katie
Badham, San Diego State University Megan
Santos, San Diego State University James
Powell, San Diego State University
Anne E. Leak, University of California at Santa Barbara
Noreen Balos, University of California at Santa Barbara
Leo Farias, California Polytechnic University at San Luis Obispo
Loren Johnson, California Polytechnic University at San Luis Obispo
Liz Walker, Tennessee Technological University
Ryan Calloway, Tennessee Technological University
Carla Moore, Tennessee Technological University
Ian Robinson, Tennessee Technological University
Rob Reab, Tennessee Technological University
Nate Reynolds, California State University at San Marcos
Lauran Gerhart, California State University at San Marcos

Unit M: Developing a Model for Magnetism
Table of Contents

Lesson #	Lesson (L) Title	Page
L1	**Modeling and the Mystery Tube**	**M-1**
L2	**Exploring Magnetic Effects**	**M-7**
Ext A[1]	Exploring the Region Around a Magnet	*online*
L3	**Developing a Model for Magnetism**	**M-19**
Ext B	Evaluating Magnetism Models	*online*
L4	**Better Model for Magnetism**	**M-29**
L5	**Explaining Phenomena Involving Magnetism**	**M-37**
L6 ED	**Engineering Design: The Maglev System**	**M-45**
L7 (optional)	**Exploring Static Electric Effects** (*only for classes not doing Unit SE*)	**M-51**

---

[1] Extensions (Ext) are online, interactive homework activities.

Purpose

When scientists try to explain what they see happening in the world around them, they construct models to help them understand why things happen as they do. In general, a scientific model is a set of connected ideas that can be used to explain phenomena that have already been observed and also guide

whether the model is good or not. We will introduce you to the scientific practice of developing, testing, and revising modeling by using a simple situation: figuring out a model to explain how the mystery tube works.

The key question for this lesson is:

How can you decide whether a model is good or not?

Developing a Model for the Mystery Tube

The mystery tube has four strings emerging from four numbered holes. (The knots (or beads) attached to each string are simply to stop the ends from passing into the tube.) Your task in this lesson is to develop a model of how these strings are arranged inside the tube, based only on observations you can make from outside the tube.

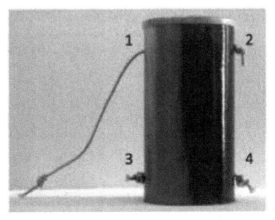

However, before you can propose an initial model, you need to have some evidence to base it on. Watch a movie **(UM L1 Movie 1)** of someone pulling the string in the upper right (labeled 2).

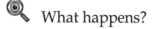 What happens?

Based on this one observation, you can construct your first model for how you think the strings are arranged inside the tube.

 Draw lines on the diagram below to show how you think the strings are arranged inside the tube. Briefly explain why you drew them as you did.

First Model

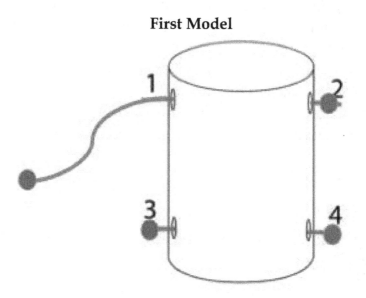

Use your first model to make a prediction. When string 3 (on lower left) is pulled, what do you expect to happen?

CQ 1-1: When string 3 (on lower left) is pulled, what do you expect to happen?

A. Nothing.
B. String 3 will get longer, but no other string will be affected.
C. String 3 will get longer and string 1 will get shorter.
D. String 3 will get longer and string 4 will be pulled tight.
E. Something else will happen.

Watch a movie **(UM L1 Movie 2)** of someone pulling string 3.

 What happens?

Did your first model account for your observation?

Second Model

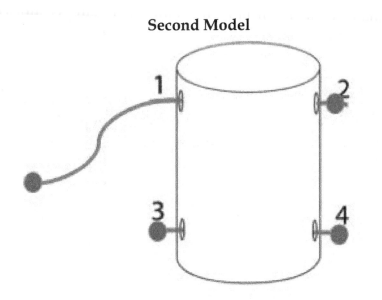

Use your second model to make a prediction. When string 4 (on lower right) is pulled, what do you expect to happen?

CQ 1-2: When string 4 (on lower right) is pulled, what do you expect to happen?

A. Nothing.
B. String 4 will get longer, but no other string will be affected.
C. String 4 will get longer and string 1 will get shorter.
D. String 4 will get longer and string 2 will get shorter.
E. Something else will happen.

Watch a movie (UM L1 Movie 3) of someone pulling string 4.

What happens?

Did your second model account for your latest observation?

If your model has accounted for all the evidence so far, then at this point you should have a 'good' model. However, if your latest observation did not match your prediction from your second model, then you need to revise your model.

Third Model

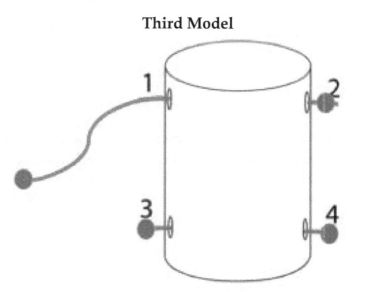

Finally, watch a movie (UM L1 Movie 4) where several strings are pulled.

Record your observations here.

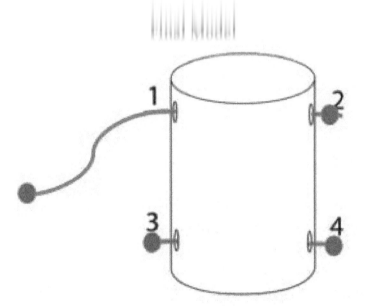

Summarizing Question

S1. Your instructor will show you several different possible models for the mystery tube.

CQ 1-3: Which of the mystery tube models shown by your instructor is closest to the one your group constructed?

A. Model A
B. Model B
C. Model C
D. Model D
E. Model E

S2. In general, in science, why is it important to make a prediction before performing a specific experiment?

The scientific practice of modeling

In the remainder of this unit and the next one, you will be developing your own models to explain phenomena involving magnetism and static electricity. Just as you practiced in this lesson with the mystery tube, the scientific practice of modeling involves proposing an initial model, testing it by making predictions, and revising it if necessary. The cycle continues until your model can 'explain' a wide range of phenomena of interest and also make accurate predictions for new situations where the model is still applicable. Scientists engage in this practice all the time.

Purpose and Materials Needed

You are no doubt familiar with some magnetic phenomena, like using a magnet to hold paper on a refrigerator door or using a compass to navigate. However, could you explain to someone else how these

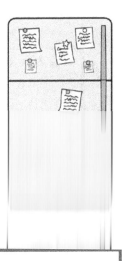

 What are some properties of magnetic interactions?

Your group's kit has the following materials that you will use for this lesson:

- Deep-dish bowl
- Disc of Styrofoam
- An envelope containing several items (see Table 1 below)
- Small magnetic compass
- Piece of tape
- Empty zippered plastic bag to use to empty the water in at the end of class
- In addition, your team should have a bottle of water.

One member in your group should get a **bar magnet** and four small **disc magnets** (or a total of four bar magnets or four of any other type of magnet) from your instructor. Another group member should pick up three nails. Keep the nails far away from the magnets.

> **When you get the magnets, keep them on the floor, far away from the nails and any other items in your kit, until you are directed to use them.**

Predictions, Observations and Making Sense

Part 1: How do magnets interact with other materials and with each other?

Do all types of objects show magnetic effects? That is, are all objects attracted to a magnet?

CQ 2-1: What kinds of materials do you think are attracted to a magnet?

A. All materials, both metals (copper, aluminum, iron, brass, etc.) and non-metals (plastic, wood, glass, etc.)
B. Only metals, but not non-metals
C. Only non-metals, but not metals
D. Only certain metals, not all metals
E. Only certain metals and non-metals, but not all of them

To find out, lay the items listed in the table below (from your envelope) on a desktop. [If materials are not available, watch a movie (**UM L2 Movie 1**).] You will also need a plastic pen or plastic ruler. **[Only test one nail. Place other nails far away from the magnet.]** Bring the bar magnet near each. For each item, record in the table whether it is attracted (A) to the magnet, repelled (R) from the magnet, or if there is no effect (O). For each case, turn the magnet around and see if you get the same effect, or if something different happens (and if so, record that in the table). Add two other items of your own choice to the table and test them.

Table I: Observations of Magnet near Objects (A, R or O)

	Wood strip	Steel paper clip	Plastic pen or ruler	Alumi-num strip	Iron nail	Copper wire	Nickel strip or wire		
Magnet									

Look over the data you recorded in Table I.

Does a magnet affect all objects? If not, which of the objects does a magnet affect?

Does it make any difference which end of the magnet is used?

 Steel is an alloy (solid mixture) of iron and carbon[1]. Based on your observations, what kinds of materials seem to be affected by a magnet?

Materials that are either attracted to a magnet or are magnets themselves are called *ferromagnetic materials*. Iron is the most common ferromagnetic

ends) together slowly, but try not to let them touch each other.

Describe what you feel as they approach each other.

Now turn **one** of the magnets around and bring them together again.

Do they behave in the same way as before, or do you feel something different? If so, what?

When scientists study the natural world, they focus their attention on different types of interactions between objects. When two objects interact, they *act on* or *influence* each other in some way. In this course, you will be studying many different types of interactions. The interactions you saw above, between two magnets and also between a magnet and a ferromagnetic material, are examples of what we will call a ***magnetic interaction***.

---

[1] Stainless steel is an alloy of steel and chromium. There are two types, one of which is affected by magnets and the other, which is not.

You have observed two examples of magnetic interactions. In one example, each end of a magnet interacts with a second magnet. In the other example, each end of a magnet interacts with a ferromagnetic material that is not itself a magnet; e.g., a steel paper clip. How are these two examples of magnetic interactions different from each other?

When you are done, put the items back into the envelope. Place the bar magnet and disc (or other) magnets back on the floor—far away from the other nails.

In the rest of this lesson, you will use iron (steel) nails to explore some important properties of the magnetic interaction.

Part 2: What happens when a nail is rubbed with a magnet?

In this experiment you will distinguish between two types of nails: those that have been rubbed with a magnet (called *rubbed*), and those that have not been rubbed with a magnet (called *unrubbed*). Initially all your nails should be *unrubbed*.

> **Please keep the bar magnet far away from the iron nails until you are directed to use it. Once you rub a nail, it is no longer "unrubbed." Please do *not* rub the nails until you are asked to do so.**

Watch the movies **(UM L2 Movie 2** and **UM L2 Movie 3) of how you should carry out the following explorations. It is important that everyone follows the same procedure.** Below are instructions that you may refer to after the movies.

To make a sensitive detector, place the dish on the table with enough water in it to fill it to a depth of about one-half inch. Place the small float in the water and put one of the **unrubbed** nails on it. The nail 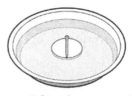 may stick out more than the one shown here in the figure. (If it does not float freely, you may need to add a little more water to the dish.)

Now make a **rubbed** nail as follows. Far away from the floating nail, pick up a second **unrubbed** nail and hold it horizontally at its head end. (The end you would hit with a hammer.) Pick up the bar magnet, hold it at right angles to the nail and slide one end of the magnet (either end is OK) **all the way from the head to the point end of the nail**.

Then lift up the bar magnet and repeat this a few more times, always sliding it in the same direction (**not** back and forth).

Record here which Pole of the magnet (N or S) you used to touch and slide

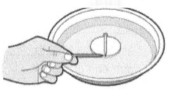

your hand and bring its tip **close to** (but not touching) the floating unrubbed nail. See the picture to the right showing that the held nail should be **horizontal** (just above and parallel to the surface of the water) and at **right angles** to the floating nail.

Always test held and floating nails this way. Do not bring the held nail downward from above (picture below to the left), and do not bring it parallel to the floating nail (picture below to the right).

Do NOT do it this way (from above)   **Do NOT do it this way (parallel)**

What, if anything, happens to the tip of the floating unrubbed nail? Is it attracted (A), repelled R), or does it show no reaction (O)? Record your observation in the appropriate box in Table II below.

Next, bring the point end of the rubbed nail near the head end of the unrubbed nail and record your observations in Table II.

Finally, bring the head end of the rubbed nail near the point end of the unrubbed nail, and then bring it near the head end of the unrubbed nail. Record both observations in Table II.

[If appropriate, you can watch a movie (UM L2 Movie 4) of these effects.]

Table II: Interactions between Rubbed and Unrubbed Nails (A, R or O)

	Point end of **unrubbed** nail	Head end of **unrubbed** nail
Point end of (held) magnet-rubbed nail		
Head end of (held) magnet-rubbed nail		

Do the two ends of the **unrubbed nail** behave the same way or differently when each end of the magnet-rubbed nail is brought nearby?

Lay the rubbed nail aside for a moment. *Imagine* that you removed the floating nail, rubbed it with the magnet in **exactly the same way** that you rubbed the other nail, and then floated it again. (**DON'T DO IT YET!**) You would then have two rubbed nails—one held and one floating.

Predict what you think would happen if you were to bring the tip of the held **rubbed** nail near the tip of the floating **rubbed** nail.

Predict what you think would happen if you were to bring the tip of the held **rubbed** nail hear the head of the floating **rubbed** nail.

Now remove the floating nail, rub it with the magnet using the **same end** of the magnet you used previously, and replace it on the floater. Then test your predictions.

Repeat the same set of four tests that you did in STEP 3 with the two

	rubbed nail	**rubbed** nail
Point end of (held) magnet-rubbed nail		
Head end of (held) magnet-rubbed nail		

Do the two ends of the magnet-rubbed floating nail behave the same way or differently when each end of the magnet-rubbed nail is brought nearby?

Based on your observations, would you claim that rubbing a nail in the way you did turned it into a magnet with two ends that behave differently? Yes or no? What evidence supports your answer?

When a nail (or any other object made of a ferromagnetic material) is rubbed with a magnet and behaves in the same way as you observed above, we say it is *magnetized*. Therefore, from now on we will refer to a 'rubbed nail' as a 'magnetized nail,' and an 'unrubbed nail' as an 'unmagnetized nail.'

Some magnetized objects retain their magnetism for very long periods of time, and we call them *permanent magnets*. The bar magnet you are using is probably made from alnico, an alloy of iron with **al**uminum, **ni**ckel and **co**balt, that is a good permanent magnet. Other ferromagnetic materials, which tend to loose their magnetism easily after being magnetized, are sometimes called *temporary magnets*.

Suppose you were to touch a magnetized nail all over with your fingers.

Do you think the nail would still be magnetized after you did this, or would it act more like an unmagnetized nail now? Why do you think so?

Now test your thinking by touching one of your magnetized nails all over with your fingers. Place it on the float and test its ends with your second magnetized nail.

Was the nail still magnetized after you touched it all over or not?

Now suppose you dropped a magnetized nail in water. Do you think the nail would still be magnetized after you did this, or not? Why do you think so?

Again, test your thinking by dropping one of your magnetized nails in your pan of water. Then place it on the float and test its ends with another magnetized nail.

Was the nail still magnetized after it was immersed in water, or not?

Your instructor will review the observations with the class. If appropriate, you can watch a movie **(UM L2 Movie 6)** of the effects.

Part 3: How are the ends of magnets and magnetized objects labeled?

Place a **magnetized** nail on the floater, making sure the other rubbed nail and the bar magnet are far away. [If your chair or table has steel legs or supports, they may affect the following observation. In that case, you should try to keep the dish away from the steel by moving it to a different part of the chair top or table, or just holding the dish in the air.] Now do the following a few times. (You may have to wait up to a half minute or so each time for the nail to settle into a stable position.)

Your instructor will point out the approximate directions for north, south, east and west. You can watch a movie **(UM L2 Movie 7)** of the effect if materials are not available.

Does the floating magnetized nail end up pointing in a different direction each time, or does it always seem to end up pointing in the same direction? If so, in which direction does the pointed end of the nail seem to 'want' to point?

CQ 2-2: Which direction is the point end of your group's magnet-rubbed nail pointing after it settles down?

A. North
B. East
C. South
D. West

Whenever a rubbed nail, or any magnet, is allowed to rotate freely without another magnet nearby, one end will always end up pointing (approximately) towards the geographical North Pole of the Earth. By mutual agreement, scientists **define** this end of the magnet as the *north-seeking pole* (or N-pole for short) of the magnet. The opposite end of the magnet, by definition, is called the *south-seeking pole* (S-pole). (Your bar magnet may already have its ends labeled as N and S to signify this.) Thus, when you rub your nail, you turn it into a magnet with a N-pole and a S-pole.

🔍 Is the tip (pointed) end of your group's floating magnetized nail a N-pole or a S-pole? What about the head end?

In your kit, you should also have a small magnetic compass. Take it out and place it on the palm of your hand, holding it far away from the magnet and the magnet-rubbed nails. The needle in the compass is made of a special ferromagnetic material that has been magnetized and retains its properties for a long time; i.e., it is a small permanent magnet.

The compass needle is free to pivot, and so one end of the needle will always point towards geographic north—and by definition, that is the N-pole of the compass needle. (Notice that, in effect, your floating magnetized nail is also a compass needle.)

🔍 Which end of **your** compass needle is a N-pole, the colored tip or the uncolored tip? (Do not rely on the labels on the compass itself. Instead, use the directions above to help you. Other groups' compasses may be different from yours.)

Part 4: How do the poles of two magnets interact with each other?

Lay your compass on the table and rotate it so that the N-pole end of the compass needle is aligned with the "N" marking (for the North direction) on the casing of the compass (as in the picture above).

Lay one of your magnetized nails on the table with its N-pole pointing towards the "E" (for East) label on the compass, and then slide it towards the compass, as shown in the picture below. [*Note: Your magnetized nail may have its N-pole at its head end, in which case you would slide its head end toward the compass.*]

Magnetized nail

🔍 What happens to the N-pole of the compass needle? Is it attracted to or

🔍 What happens to the N-pole of the compass needle now? What about the S-pole of the compass needle?

🧩 Do like poles (N-N or S-S) of the magnetized nail and compass needle attract or repel each other? Do unlike poles (N-S or S-N) attract or repel each other?

Check your conclusions with at least one other group to make sure you all agree. If not, repeat the observations. If appropriate, you can watch a movie **(UM L2 Movie 8)** of the effects.

Your statement about how like and unlike Poles interact with each other is known as the *Law of Magnetic Poles*.

As you have seen in this lesson, the two ends of a magnetized nail behave differently when near another magnetized nail. Because of this property, we say that a magnetized nail is '*two-ended*.' On the other hand, since both ends of the unmagnetized nail behave the same when near another magnetized nail, we say that it is '*one-ended*.'

Summarizing Questions

S1. An elementary school student asks you for advice about a science project she is doing on recycling. She suggests that a large permanent magnet could be used to separate metals from non-metals in the trash passing through a recycling station. What do you think of this idea?

S2. In this lesson you magnetized a nail by rubbing its surface with a magnet. Do you think that whatever causes a nail to be magnetic also lies on its surface, or is it inside the nail? What evidence supports your thinking?

Purpose

In the previous lesson you discovered that magnet-rubbed (magnetized) iron nails behave differently from unrubbed (unmagnetized) iron nails. Thus, rubbing the nail with a magnet must change the nail in some way. But *how* does it change the nail? To answer this question, you need to develop a model: a picture and description of what you think is going on inside the nail.

scientists make their predictions based on their model, they (or other scientists) perform the experiments. If the predictions are **confirmed** through the new experiments, the scientists retain their model because it can explain their new observations. However, if the results of the new experiments differ from the predictions, scientists use the new evidence to **revise** their model so it can explain the new set of observations (as well as the previous observations). Then they use their revised model to make new predictions. They develop confidence in their model only after it can be used repeatedly to make predictions that are confirmed in new experiments. A critically important activity of scientists is to develop, test, and revise models.

 How can you develop a model for magnetism?

Predictions, Observations and Making Sense

Part 1: What is your initial model for magnetism?

A **good model** in science meets the following criteria:

- The model (the drawing and the written part) should be clear and understandable. If you use 'symbols' in your drawing of a model, you should describe in words what the nature of those symbols are; that is, what they represent.
- The model should be plausible and causal; that is, it should make sense according to your own ideas about cause and effect. In the case of a model for magnetism, what you show happening when a nail is rubbed with a magnet should both make sense and explicitly indicate how moving the magnet along the surface of the nail causes something to happen in or on the nail.
- The model should account for (explain) <u>all</u> the observable evidence and not contradict any of that evidence.
- The model should guide accurate predictions about what would happen in new experiments.

You know from previous observations that a magnet rubbed nail becomes magnetized and is *two-ended*. Imagine that you rub the unrubbed nail in such a way that its point end becomes a North Pole. [You can always test this using the compass.] Below are two drawings of the nail, representing its state before and after rubbing with a magnet.

?🔯 **Individually**, sketch what you think might be different about the iron nail in these two conditions (unmagnetized and magnetized). Think about what entities might be inside the nail, and what might happen to them in the process of rubbing with a magnet, that causes the nail to become magnetized and two-ended. Use symbols like + and -, N and S, or some combination of them to represent the entities. Do not use abstract symbols, like arrows or rectangles, since it would be difficult to interpret what they mean. To make things concrete, assume you rubbed the nail so its point is a North Pole and its head is a South Pole.

Your first <u>individual</u> model:

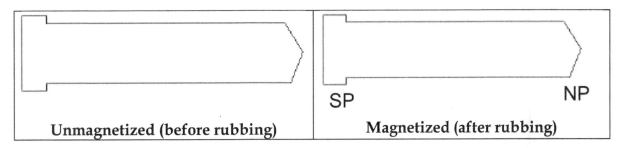

Unmagnetized (before rubbing)	SP NP
	Magnetized (after rubbing)

Describe <u>your</u> initial *model* in words, in particular how the "Magnetized"

Each member of your group should now describe her initial model to the other group members by carefully describing what the entities are and how they become rearranged in some way (if at all) when the nail is magnetized. Then try to decide on one model that represents the group's 'best' thinking.

Sketch your **group's best initial model**.

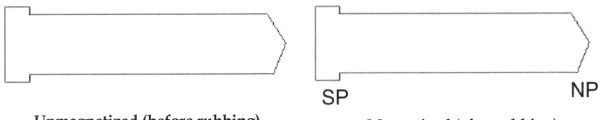

Unmagnetized (before rubbing)

SP   NP

Magnetized (after rubbing)

Discuss within your group how the model can 'explain' why rubbing an unmagnetized nail with a magnet results in it becoming *magnetized*.

🧩 Discuss within your group how the model represents that an unmagnetized nail is *one-ended* (both ends behave the same way), but a magnetized nail is *two-ended* (the two ends behave differently).

CQ 3-1: Which is most similar to your group's initial model?

A. Plus (+) and minus (-) entities are randomly spread throughout the unrubbed nail; rubbing separates them to the two halves of the nail.
B. North (N) and South (S) entities are randomly spread throughout the unrubbed nail; rubbing separates them to the two halves of the nail
C. Some other type of entities are inside the nail; rubbing causes them to re-orient or change in some other way than being separated to the two halves of the nail.
D. Something different from above.

In the past we have found that most groups at this point suggest a model that has the following features. Inside the unrubbed nail there are two different types of entities, either plusses and minuses or norths and souths, and the individual entities are scattered randomly throughout the nail. During the act of sliding the magnet across the nail, the two types of entities separate from each other; one type goes towards one end, and the other type goes towards the other end. Because this initial model is so common, we give it its own name: the *separation model*.

For groups that have invented some form of a separation model, some groups have probably used + and – symbols as the entities, and other groups may have used N and S symbols as the entities. For consistency in comparing models, it would be a good idea to agree on one set of symbols. Batteries have + and - labels at their ends, and magnets have N and S labels at their ends (poles). Since we are focusing on magnetic effects here, not electric effects, to keep things simple, we suggest everyone uses N and S labels in their model (if appropriate).

Re-draw your group's initial model **using N and S labels** for the entities (if appropriate). You might also decide to adopt a different model from your original one, and that's fine; just draw it below.

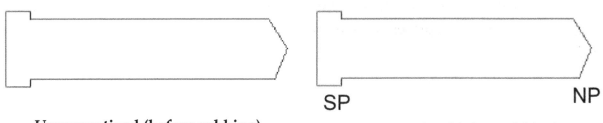

Unmagnetized (before rubbing)

SP   NP

Magnetized (after rubbing)

Part 2: Testing the initial model

experiments. You will be testing that criterion in this part of the lesson.

Important: When you make predictions, you <u>must</u> base them on your <u>current</u> model. Do <u>not</u> change your model as a result of just thinking about the situation, because then you are not testing your model. If the outcome of the experiment turns out to be <u>exactly</u> what you had predicted, then don't modify your model. On the other hand, if the outcome is different from your prediction, even in small ways, then you need to consider how to revise your model. Finally, for this process to be useful, the predictions you make should be precise, not vague and general. Only then will the experiment really test your model appropriately.

To help your group make a prediction based on its initial model (rather than on some other intuition), you should use the following procedure. On a separate piece of paper draw a large version of your current model for a **magnetized nail**. Next draw a thick vertical line through the exact middle of your model drawing, and then tear your drawing in half, exactly along that line. You should end up with two drawings, each representing half of the magnetized nail. Separate these two halves on your table.

Copy your drawings of the two halves of the model below, showing your model's representation of the two halves of the nail.

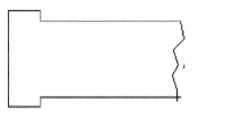

Head half of magnetized nail

Point half of magnetized nail

Now look at the entities inside each half piece and answer these questions **based on your model drawing**.

Does your model of the **head half piece** (on the left) suggest that it, **by itself,** is one-ended, two-ended, or something different? (One-ended means that the entities are the same on each end, suggesting each end would behave the same. If you think something different, try to describe it in words.)

Does your model of the **point half piece** (on the right) suggest that it, **by itself,** is one-ended, two-ended, or something different? (If different, try to describe it in words.)

Your drawings above represent what your model suggests would be in each piece of a magnetized nail that is cut in half. You will now use these to make a **prediction** about what you would find if you actually did this and tested each piece of the cut nail separately.

CQ 3-2: What does your torn-in-half model drawing predict would happen if the actual rubbed nail were cut in half? [Assume that the act of cutting does not rearrange the entities in any way. They stay where they were before cutting.]

A. The head half piece would now be one-ended, and the point half piece would also be one-ended (but with opposite types of entities).

B. The head half piece would now be two-ended, and the point half piece would also be two-ended (each piece has different kinds of entities at

Watch a movie (UM L3 Movie 1) from which you can determine whether your prediction was accurate or not. In the movie, the person first magnetizes the nail by rubbing it with a bar magnet. He then brings first the tip of the rubbed nail, and then the head of the rubbed nail, near the E-label on the compass.

What does the compass needle do in each case?

Is the point end of the rubbed nail a North Pole or a South Pole?

Do the observations suggest that the rubbed nail is two-ended, one-ended, or something else?

Next the person carefully cuts the nail exactly in half. He will now test each half piece.

🔍 What happens when he brings each end of the head half piece near the E-label on the compass?

🧩 Do the observations suggest that the head half piece is two-ended, one-ended, or something else?

🔍 What happens when he brings each end of the point half piece near the E-label on the compass?

🧩 Do the observations suggest that the point half piece is two-ended, one-ended, or something else?

🧩 What can you conclude from this experiment?

> **CQ 3-3**: When a rubbed nail is cut in half, what can you conclude?
>
> A. Each half piece is still two-ended.
> B. Each half piece is one-ended.
> C. One half piece is one-ended, and the other is two-ended.
> D. Conclude something else. [Describe what.]

Your group used its initial model to make a prediction about what would happen if the rubbed nail were cut in half. If what actually happened differs from your prediction, then your group needs to revise its initial model.

🧩 Does your group's initial model need to be revised: yes or no?

If you answered 'yes,' before you revise it we want to provide you with some additional evidence to guide you.

Watch the following movie **(UM L3 Movie 2).** The person starts, as before, by magnetizing the nail so its point end is a North Pole. The person will now cut the rubbed nail into two **unequal** pieces, one longer, one shorter. He'll then bring each end of each piece near the E-label on the compass.

What happens when each end of the *longer piece* is brought near the E-label on the compass?

Do the observations suggest that the longer piece is two-ended, one-ended, or something else?

Do the observations suggest that the shorter piece is two-ended, one-ended, or something else?

What can you conclude from this experiment? When a rubbed nail is cut in unequal length pieces, is each piece still two-ended, one-ended, or something else (describe)?

The person in the movie could have cut the rubbed nail *anywhere* along its length. In each case, however, you would have concluded that each cut piece is two-ended.

Your group now needs to be creative and revise your initial model so it could account for <u>all</u> the new evidence.

Your group's revised model:

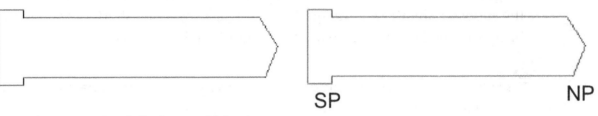

SP

NP

Unmagnetized (before rubbing)   **Magnetized (after rubbing)**

How does your revised model account for the observation that cutting a magnetized nail **anywhere along its length** would still give two pieces that are both *two-ended*? (If it cannot account for this, say why not.)

One member of your group should take a picture of the group's revised model with a cell phone camera and email it according to your instructor's directions. On the subject line, type "Group N **revised** model," where N represents your group number.

Summarizing Question

CQ 3-4: Can your group's revised model explain the observation that cutting the magnetized nail anywhere along its length will produce two pieces that are each magnetized (two-ended)?

A. Yes, it can.
B. No, it cannot.
C. We are not sure.

Your instructor may share some of the class' revised models. You may wish to copy down some of these other models if you think they will be helpful.

LESSON 4: Better Model for Magnetism

Purpose and Materials Needed

In the previous lesson your group created an initial model for magnetism that could explain the two-endedness property of magnetized nails. Then you used the model to make a prediction. Most likely, the experimental results were not what you had predicted, and you needed to revise your model. By the end of the lesson, you realized that a successful model

reconceptualize their model. For example, in the case of the model for magnetism, perhaps you need to think differently about what kinds of entities are inside the nail. Thinking in terms of separate N and S entities might not be fruitful. In this lesson you will gather evidence that could help you reconceptualize your model of magnetism; that is, help you think again about what kinds of entities might be inside of a nail, and what happens to them when the nail is rubbed with a magnet.

How can you develop a better model for magnetism?

Predictions, Observations and Making Sense

Part 1: Thinking about the effects of collections of magnets or magnetized nails

A magnetized nail can interact with an unmagnetized nail (attracting each end), but an unmagnetized nail does not interact with another unmagnetized nail (there are no effects). This suggests that whatever entities are inside the nail, in an unmagnetized nail these entities collectively produce no magnetic effects outside the nail. On the other hand, rubbing the nail causes something to happen to these entities so that collectively they do produce magnetic effects outside the nail.

From the last lesson you can infer that the entities inside the nail cannot be separate N and S entities that rearrange themselves when the nail is rubbed, because that kind of model cannot explain all the observations. So perhaps the *entities* need to be something *different*. The following movies will provide evidence that could help you re-think about what the entities might be, and how they might behave when the nail is magnetized.

To begin, watch a movie **(UM L4 Movie 1)** of a compass with its north pole pointing towards the N-label on the compass housing. This is the zero degree mark. Previously, you had seen that a single magnetized nail placed near the E-label on the compass housing could cause the compass needle to deflect. In this movie, the person rubs four nails identically to magnetize them the same way, and places them close to the E-label on the compass housing. The needle should rotate, suggesting that the combination of four magnetized nails produce a significant magnetic effect.

Are the point ends of the four nails North Poles or a South Poles? How do you know?

Do four magnetized nails all arranged the same way produce a larger, smaller, or about the same rotation of the compass needle as a single magnetized nail?

The four nails have their N-poles all aligned, pointing in the same direction, and the combination produces a magnetic effect in the area away from the nails (causing the compass needle to rotate). Does the orientation of the poles make any difference? What would happen if two of the nails were turned around, so their N-poles pointed in the opposite direction to the other two nails?

C. It would rotate less, or not at all.

Why do you think so?

Watch the movie **(UM L4 Movie 2)** of what happens.

Describe what happens.

Can a combination of four magnetized nails cancel out (or almost cancel out) each other's effect? If so, under what conditions would that happen?

In the next movie **(UM L4 Movie 3)**, the experimenter grabs ten bar magnets and arranges them so all the North Poles are pointing in the same direction. He then lowers the collection of magnets into a pile of paper clips.

🔍 Describe what happens.

CQ 4-2: Imagine the person changed the orientation of half the bar magnets, so half had their North Poles pointing one way and the other half had their North Poles pointing the other way, and then lowered this new collection of bar magnets into a different pile of paper clips. Would the combination of ten magnets pick up about the same number of paper clips, many more, or many fewer, or none at all?

A. About the same number
B. Many more
C. Many fewer, or none at all

⚙️ Why do you think so?

Watch the movie **(UM L4 Movie 4)** of what happens.

🔍 Describe what happens.

Next, watch a movie **(UM L4 Movie 5)** of a computer simulation that models what happens when small magnets are oriented different ways. The simulation uses a meter that measures how strongly the combination of magnets would influence a nearby compass needle (or another magnet) placed where the meter is located. Pay attention to what happens to the meter reading as more magnets are added, with their poles all aligned.

🔍 Record the value of the meter readings in the different arrangements.

Next, watch the movie **(UM L4 Movie 6)** of what happens when the orientation of the

As more magnets are added in combination, with their poles all pointing in the same direction, does the strength of the magnetic effect increase, decrease, or remain about the same?

If several magnets in a group have their poles oriented in *random directions*, does that arrangement produce a stronger magnetic effect or a weaker magnetic effect than if the magnets were all oriented in the same direction?

What can you conclude from this? Fill in the following:

So, a group of magnets can collectively produce a large magnetic effect or little or no magnetic effect, depending on how the magnets are oriented with respect to each other. If their North Poles all point in the same (or nearly the same) direction, there would be _____ magnetic effect. On the other hand, if their North Poles point in all different directions (i.e. randomly oriented), there would be _____ magnetic effect.

So, assuming you start with a bunch of magnets with their North Poles randomly oriented, how could you change their orientation to make them all aligned? We'll explore that in the next part of this lesson.

Part 2: Changing the orientation of magnets

In the previous part, you concluded that if you have several magnets, the combination could produce either a large magnetic effect or a little or no magnetic effect, depending on the relative orientations of the magnet poles. So, if you have a combination of magnets with their poles randomly oriented, what might you do to cause all the poles of the magnets to align? To start simple, consider just a single magnet.

Imagine you have a magnet that is fixed in position and can only pivot (rotate) around its center. What do you think would happen to the pivoting magnet if another magnet were dragged above it from left to right, as shown in the picture below?

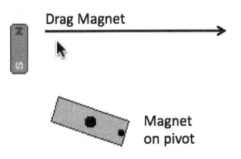

Watch the movie **(UM L4 Movie 7)** of this situation.

Describe what happens to the magnet on the pivot as the South Pole of the other magnet is dragged from left to right.

Which end of the magnet on the pivot is its North Pole: the end with the small dot or the end without the small dot? How do you know?

Of course, if we started with a collection of many magnets, each free to rotate about its own pivot, then we could change the orientation of all the magnets by dragging a magnet across the collection.

Part 3: A final model for magnetism

Hopefully, your investigations in Parts 1 and 2 of this lesson gave you new insight into what you could imagine might be the

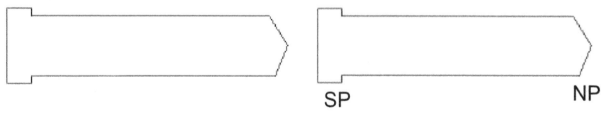

- *An unrubbed nail produces no magnetic effects (it's unmagnetized).*
- *A rubbed nail is magnetized, producing a large magnetic effect.*
- *A rubbed (magnetized) nail is two-ended; that is, each end behaves differently.*
- *A magnetized nail cut anywhere along its length produces two nail pieces that are each magnetized, but each piece produces a weaker magnetic effect than the whole nail.*

Your group's final model:

Unmagnetized (before rubbing)

SP   NP

Magnetized (after rubbing)

One member of your group should take a picture of your group's final model and e-mail it according to your instructor's directions. On the subject line, type "Group N final model," where N is your group number.

🧩 Your group should spend a few minutes going over each of the four bullet points above and discussing how your group's model can "explain" each of them.

Summarizing Question

Your instructor will help the class develop a **consensus final model** that is supported by all the evidence collected so far, and that everyone could use to explain magnetic phenomena.

Purpose and Key Question

By the end of Lesson 4, the class reached consensus on a model of magnetism that could explain all the observations that have been made thus far. We refer to this model as an **alignment model**, and we list its basic features here. (1) Inside ferromagnetic materials, there are a large number of entities that behave *like* tiny magnets. (2) In ⟨text obscured⟩ ...... of a permanent magnet slides across the ferromagnetic material, it attracts the North Poles of every tiny magnet (and repels the South Poles), causing each tiny magnet to pivot (rotate) in place so that all the North Poles end up pointing in the same direction; that is, all the tiny magnets become aligned. In this case, the magnetic effects due to all of the magnets reinforce each other. Thus, the entire material produces a large magnetic effect. It is also assumed that materials that do not exhibit magnetic effects do not contain these tiny magnets.

In this lesson, we will apply the alignment model to make some predictions and to explain some new observations. Remember, a *good* model can do both.

> *How can you use the alignment model of magnetism to explain some phenomena?*

Your team will need the following:
▶ Several iron nails (at least four)
▶ Paper clips
▶ Small magnetic compass
▶ Small bar magnet (keep far away from everything else)

Predictions, Observations and Making Sense

Part 1: How can you rub a nail to ensure a particular end is a North Pole?

Based on the alignment model, **predict two different ways** that you could rub a nail with a magnet so that the point end of the nail becomes a North Pole. Discuss with your group and write your predictions below. Briefly indicate your reasoning. [You can use either end of the bar magnet to do the rubbing, and you can rub the nail in either direction, from head to point or the other way.]

After making your two predictions, try it! Use your compass and apply the Law of Magnetic Poles to check if your nail tip is indeed a North Pole for each case. Record your observations below. You should draw pictures showing which direction you rub the nail, and which end of the magnet you are using.

Consider the following four different ways you might rub the nail:

      I. Rub the North end of the magnet from the head to the point end of the nail.

      II. Rub the North end of the magnet from the point to the head end of the nail.

      III. Rub the South end of the magnet from the head to the point end of the nail.

      IV. Rub the South end of the magnet from the point to the head end of the nail.

CQ 5-1: Which of the above procedures will produce a magnetized nail with its point end a North Pole?

A. I and II
B. I and III
C. I and IV
D. II and III
E. II and IV

If appropriate, you can watch a movie **(UM L5 Movie 1)** of the various ~~~~

~~~~ ~~~~ ~~~~

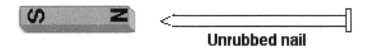

~~~~ ~~~~ ~~~~ a S-pole. But suppose, instead of sliding the N-pole of the magnet across the nail, you just held its North Pole <u>near</u> the tip of the nail?

Unrubbed nail

CQ 5-2: If you hold the N-pole of a bar magnet <u>near</u> the tip of an unmagnetized (unrubbed) nail, without touching it, what do you think will happen to the nail?

A. It would remain unrubbed; that is, it would not be magnetized.
B. It would be magnetized, with the tip a N-pole and the head a S-pole.
C. It would be magnetized, with the tip a S-pole and the head a N-pole.
D. Its tip would act like a N-pole, but its head would not have a Pole.
E. Its tip would act like a S-pole, but its head would not have a Pole.

Explain your reasoning.

To test your prediction, lay the compass on the desktop. Then hold an *unmagnetized* (unrubbed) nail on the table with its tip pointed towards the E-label on a compass, as shown below. The tip should be very close to the compass, but not touching it. The compass needle should *not* rotate, indicating the nail is unmagnetized. [If it does rotate, get another nail and try again.]

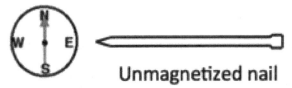

Unmagnetized nail

Next, remove the compass and hold the tip of the nail about 0.5 cm from the N-pole of a magnet for a few seconds. *Be sure to hold both the nail and the magnet so they don't move towards each other and touch. If they do touch, start over with another unrubbed nail.* See picture.

Initially Unmagnetized nail

Then place the nail near the compass again as shown above.

🔍 What happens to the compass needle?

Turn the nail around so its head end is near the E-label on the compass.

🔍 Now what happens to the compass needle?

🧩 What do these two observations suggest happened to the nail? Is it magnetized, with both a N-pole and a S-pole? If so, which end is its N-pole and which end is its S-pole?

If appropriate, you can watch a movie (**UM L5 Movie 2**) of this effect.

Next hold the point end of the **same** (now magnetized) nail about 0.5 cm from the **South Pole** of the bar magnet for a few seconds.

Already magnetized nail

Then bring the point end of the nail near the E-label of the compass.

🔍 What happens to the compass needle?

🧩 Is the nail magnetized? If so, is its point end a North Pole or a South Pole? What about its head end?

🧩 Do these results suggest that a nail can be magnetized without touching a magnet?

🧩 Can a magnetized nail with certain poles have its poles easily switched?

Recall that some ferromagnetic materials (e.g., steel, which is an alloy containing iron) can be easily magnetized and can easily have their poles reversed (as you saw above with the nails). It is also relatively easy to demagnetize them. Such materials, when magnetized, are known as *temporary magnets*. A magnetized nail is an example of a temporary magnet. Certain other kinds of ferromagnetic materials (e.g., alnico) can be made into *permanent magnets*. These materials are difficult to magnetize, but once magnetized, they are difficult to demagnetize and they retain their pole orientation for a very long time. Bar magnets and compass needles are examples of permanent magnets.

In the following diagram, use the alignment model to explain why the nail becomes magnetized when held near a magnet. First draw the entities inside the unmagnetized nail (top nail), and then draw what happens to them when the nail is near the magnet (bottom nail).

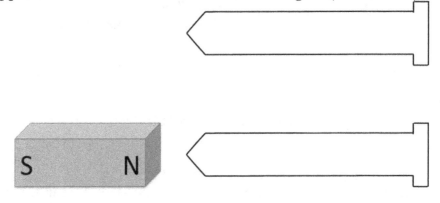

What caused the entities to re-orient themselves? Be specific and make use of the Law of Magnetic Poles.

Part 3: Why does a magnet attract unmagnetized (ferromagnetic) objects?

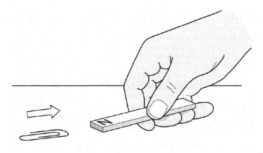

Remember from Lesson 2 that you observed either end of the magnet attracted a paper clip. Watch a movie (**UM L5 Movie 3**) of this effect.

What happens to the paper clip?

🧩 Explain why this happens by drawing a set of diagrams (the paper clip before and after the magnet is held nearby), and then writing a few sentences. [Hint: You can think of the paper clip as being similar to an unmagnetized nail.]

In a similar way, you can explain why refrigerator magnets stick to steel refrigerators (steel contains iron), or how the Etch-A-Sketch toys work (a magnet attracts tiny particles of iron).

CQ 5-3: Suppose you bring a magnet near an object and you observe that the object is attracted towards the magnet. What can you conclude about the properties of the object from this <u>one</u> observation?

A. The object is ferromagnetic and was already magnetized before the magnet was brought near.
B. The object is ferromagnetic but was not magnetized before the magnet was brought near.
C. Either A or B could have been true.
D. The object is not ferromagnetic.
E. You cannot conclude anything from this one observation.

Part 4: What happens when you heat a magnetized object?

Imagine you rubbed an iron nail with a bar magnet, and then brought it near the E-label on a compass. You observed the compass needle had rotated a certain amount.

CQ 5-4: Suppose you then heated the magnetized nail with a very hot torch for several seconds. After the nail cooled some, what would you observe the compass needle do if you then brought it near the E-label of the compass?

A. It would rotate the same amount as it did before it was heated.
B. It would rotate much more than it did before it was heated.
C. It would rotate much less than it did before it was heated.

Why do you think so?

Watch a movie **(UM L5 Movie 4).** Describe what happens.

In terms of the alignment model, what do you think happened to the tiny magnets when the nail was heated?

The Maglev System: An Engineering Design Challenge

Maglev train in Japan (Image Courtesy of Yosemite, GNU Free Documentation License.)

The maglev train has long been the holy grail of ground transportation. Levitating above steel rails, maglev trains need no wheels and have no friction with the track, resulting in an ultra-fast and ultra-quiet ride. So far they're also very expensive. Counting a planned Tokyo-to-Osaka leg, the Japanese maglev project is expected to cost upwards of $100 billion. If that sounds prohibitive, consider that the United States spends significantly more than that on highways in a single year. And while a highway might get you from Los Angeles to San Francisco in six hours if you're lucky, a maglev train like the one Japan's building could theoretically do it in an hour and 15 minutes. In fact, California has been trying to build a Los Angeles-to-San Francisco high-speed rail line for some 30 years, but the fight for funding has been tooth-and-nail. The state is now slated to have a 220-mph train up and running by 2028—but that's just a conventional bullet train, the kind Japan has had for decades. There were once plans for a California-Nevada maglev train, but they never left the station, and the money for planning them ended up being reallocated to a highway project. (*Future Tense*, November 30, 2012[1])

---

[1] By Will Oremus (2012). Why can't we have a 300-MPH floating train like Japan? Future Tense: The Citizens Guide to the Future. *Retrieved from:* http://www.slate.com/blogs/future_tense/2012/11/30/japan_s_300_mph_maglev_train_why_can_t_the_us_build_high_speed_rail.html.

Although it's true that the US is falling behind other countries in technological accomplishments, a renewed focus on engineering as a part of science education could make a difference, at least in the next generation (which is why the new standards are called the Next Generation Science Standards[2]).

Beginning to use the engineering design process to design a solution to a problem

The engineering design process in the Next Generation Science Standards involves three stages: (1) Defining and delimiting an engineering problem (or challenge); (2) Developing possible solutions; (3) Optimizing the design solution. In this initial engineering design lesson, we will define and delimit the engineering problem for you and you will sketch out just one possible solution, so you will not need to consider optimizing the solution. Finally, you will also be asked to use your understanding of magnetism to address some issues regarding an actual maglev train.

Your engineering problem is to sketch out the design of a simple system where an object can move a certain distance while floating above the surface. The system will represent a simple model of the maglev train. The object will be a small box that represents the train. The object will move inside a long box from one end to the other (following a gentle push) without touching the bottom (that is, it floats above the bottom of the box). The bottom of the box represents the train tracks.

1. You will need to include magnets in your solution, so you go into a store that sells a wide variety of magnets. You are looking for strips of magnetic material you can lay along the bottom of the box that you might use in your design of the model. The sales person gives you two choices. Which do you choose and why?

---

[2] NGSS Lead States (2013). *Next Generation Science Standards: Practices, Core Ideas, and Crosscutting Concepts.* Washington, DC: National Academy Press.

a. Strips that are magnetized so the top surface is one pole and the bottom surface is the other pole. (Below is a side view.)

N (Top)

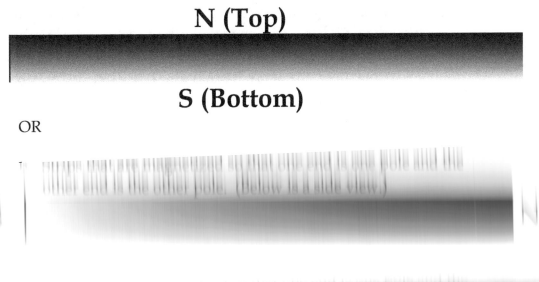

S (Bottom)

OR

CQ 6-1. Which type of magnetic strips would you choose?

A. Strips that are magnetized so the top surface is one pole and the bottom surface is a different pole.

B. Strips that are magnetized so that one end is one pole and the other end is a different pole.

C. Both would work equally well

---

2. Be creative and draw a detailed diagram of a possible model maglev train system, consisting of a long box (representing the tracks), magnets, and a small box representing the 'train.' The 'train' should float above the bottom of the box. When you give the box a gentle push, it should move from one end of the box to the other without touching the bottom. Label all parts of your system, including where the magnets or magnetic strips are located and how they are arranged (which way the poles are oriented).

3. Using ideas from the unit on magnetism, explain how your model will work.

4. Imagine that you've gone to Japan and you've been invited to ride in the control room of a maglev train. You're traveling at 300 miles per hour and one of the engineers reads a gauge that says one of the magnets under the train has cracked. Should you worry? Why or why not? [Use ideas from the magnetism unit to justify your answer.]

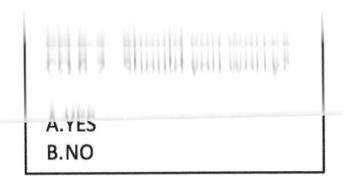

A.YES
B.NO

5. A radio call reports that catastrophe was narrowly averted when a fire on the line 50 miles ahead was put out. The crew laughs about it and assures you not to worry, that you will make it to Osaka on time. What do you say to them? [Use ideas from the magnetism unit to justify your answer.]

CQ 6-3. Should you worry?

A.YES
B.NO

Purpose

In the previous lessons you explored some magnetic effects and then went on to develop a model that explains these effects in terms of tiny entities within magnetic materials. You are also likely familiar with some other phenomena, usually associated with *static electricity*, like the 'static cling' by which

What are some properties of interactions involving electrified objects, and how do they compare with interactions involving magnetic objects?

Predictions, Observations and Making Sense

Part 1: What kinds of materials can be involved in static electric effects?

In a previous lesson you found that only certain materials could interact with a magnet. Will it be only these same materials that interact with electrified objects, or will different materials show static electric effects? What do you think?

CQ 7-1: What kinds of materials do you think can be involved in static electric effects?

A. All materials, both metals (copper, aluminum, iron, brass, etc.) and non-metals (plastic, wood, glass, etc.)

B. Only metals, but not non-metals

C. Only non-metals, but not metals

D. Only certain metals, not all metals

E. Only certain metals and non-metals, but not all of them

To find out, watch a movie **(UM L7 Movie 1),** where the experimenter will first lay one piece of tape on the table (labeled B tape), and lay a second piece of tape on top of it (labeled T-tape). The two pieces of tape will then be held up by their ends and ripped apart. This process will 'electrify' each piece of tape.

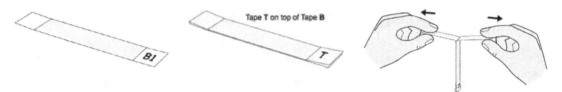

Next, different objects will be brought near the T-tape and the B-tape and you should observe what happens. Is the tape attracted (A) to the object, repelled (R) from it, or does nothing happen (O)? Record your observations in the following table.

Table I: Observations of Electrified Tapes near Objects (A, R or O)

	Wooden strip	Iron nail	Plastic pen	Aluminum foil strip	Copper wire	Nickel strip	Finger
B-tape							
T-tape							

What do your observations show about what types of materials can interact with electrified objects?

How do these results compare with what types of materials can interact with magnetized objects?

When Benjamin Franklin experimented with electrified objects, he imagined them as containing some type of electrical 'fluid' and so said they were 'charged' (as in 'charge [fill] your glasses for a toast') when describing them. While Franklin's use of 'charged' is probably different from the sense in which most people today think of it, we still use his terminology. Thus, from now on we will refer to electrified objects as being 'charged' with static electricity.

Part 2: How do electrically charged objects interact with each other?

In Part 1 you saw what happens when uncharged objects are brought near charged objects. But what would happen if the two charged tapes (B and T) were brought near each other?

Do you think they would behave like two magnets, which attract or repel depending on which ends/faces are brought close, or would they behave

the ends/faces were close to each other, they would then repel if one of the ends/faces were turned around.

B. It would not be like two magnets. If two ends/faces attracted or repelled each other, they would do the same thing if one of the ends/faces were turned around.

C. They would not react to each other.

To find out, watch a movie (UM L7 Movie 2). In this movie, the experimenter will prepare two charged tapes as he did in the previous movie, bring each side of each tape (B-tape and T-tape) near each other, and then turn the tapes around.

What happened when the two non-sticky sides of the B and T tapes initially approached each other? Did they attract, repel, or was there no reaction?

What happened when one of the tapes was turned around, and the B and T tapes were again brought near each other?

What happened when the other tape was turned around so both sticky sides faced each other?

🧩 Do the results depend which sides are tested, or does the same thing always happen?

🧩 How does this behavior of two charged tapes compare to the behavior of two magnetized nails you saw in previous lessons?

🧩 In the magnetism lessons you concluded that a magnetized object is *two-ended*. Based on your observations from the movie, would you conclude that a charged object is *one-ended* or *two-ended*? How do you know?

Part 3: How many types of charge are there?

You have seen that when peeling apart two tapes, each tape becomes charged with static electricity. But is there only one type of charge, or are there more than one and if so, how many are there?

🤔 Imagine two pairs of tapes were each charged as shown previously (call them T1/B1 and T2/B2). If you then brought tapes T1 and T2 together, what do you think would happen?

CQ 7-3: If the T1 and T2 tapes from two separate pairs of charged tapes were brought back toward each other, what do you think would happen?

A. They would attract each other.
B. They would repel each other.
C. They would not react to each other.

Watch a movie (**UM L7 Movie 3**) of an experiment in which two pairs of B and T tapes are charged and then brought toward each other in various combinations.

🔍 Record the results of all the tests in Table II below. (Enter **A** for attract, **R** for repel, or **O** for no reaction.)

Table II: Observations with Charged Tapes

	B2	T2
B1		

with each other?

Finally, we will check whether the ideas you have developed about charges using the pairs of tapes also apply to objects charged by rubbing them together. Watch a movie (**UM L7 Movie 4**) in which a balloon is rubbed against a person's hair and is brought back close to the hair again. Then the rubbed balloon is brought near charged T and B tapes.

🔍 What happened when the rubbed balloon was brought back towards the hair?

🧩 What does this observation suggest about the charges on the rubbed balloon and the rubbed hair? Are they the same or different?

🔍 What happened when the rubbed balloon was brought near the B-tape? What happened when it was brought near the T-tape?

Based on these observations, does the rubbed balloon have the same charge as the T-tape or the B-tape? How do you know?

Summarizing Questions

S1. Use evidence from this lesson to answer the following question.

> **CQ 7-4: How many types of charge are there and how do they interact?**
>
> A. There is only one type of charge. All charged objects attract each other.
> B. There is only one type of charge. All charged objects repel each other.
> C. There are two types of charge. Like charges repel and unlike charges attract.
> D. There are two types of charge. Like charges attract and unlike charges repel.

S2. Answer the following question based on your current understanding of what happens when objects are charged by rubbing or peeling.

> **CQ 7-5: What happens when two objects are charged by rubbing or peeling?**
>
> A. Both objects have the same type of charge.
> B. One object has only one type of charge. The other object has only the other type of charge.
> C. Both objects have both types of charge, but there are different amounts of each type on each object.

Law of Electric Charges

The evidence from the movies you observed in this lesson support what is known as the *Law of Electric Charges: There are two types of charge. Like charges repel and unlike charges attract.* This is similar in form to the Law of Magnetic Poles. However, as you concluded from the experiments in this lesson, although the forms of the two laws are similar, magnetized objects and charged objects behave differently, suggesting that the explanations (or models) for the two phenomena are different.